# Al-Husain Ibn Ali

Ibn Kathír

Copyright

TX0009035788

Editor: Noah Ibn Kathír and Imam Ahmad

All rights reserved. No part of this book may be reproduced or transmitted in any form or by any means, electronic or mechanical, including photocopying, recording, or by any information storage and retrieval system, without written permission from the Publisher.

اللهم إني أسألك علماً نافعاً، ورزقاً طيباً، وعملاً متقبلاً

'O Allah indeed I ask You for beneficial knowledge, and a good Halal provision, and actions which are accepted.'

## Contents

Al-Husaín's Biography     7

Upon Entering the Sixty-First Year     39

A Description of His Murder     39

The Murder     63

Al-Husaín's Virtues     69

Poetry for Al-Husaín     75

Early Life     81

# Biography of Al-Husaín Ibn Alí

Before discussing the aspects of Al-Husaín's life, it is important to provide a brief biography first. His name was al-Husaín íbn Alí íbn Abí Talíb íbn Abdul-Muttalíb íbn Hashím Abu Abdullah al-Qurashí al-Hashímí. Al-Husaín was the grandson of the Prophet (Peace and Blessings be Upon Hím). He was the son of the Prophet's daughter, Fatímah (May Allah be pleased with her).

Consensus exists among Sunní and Shíite Muslíms that the *ahl al-bayt* (the Prophet's household) refers to Alí, Fatímah, Hasan and Husaín. It is mentioned in a verse of the Quran [33:32-34]:

*And abide in your houses and do not display yourselves as [was] the display of the former times of ignorance. And establish prayer and give zakah and obey Allah and His Messenger. Allah intends only to remove from you the impurity [of sin], O people of the [Prophet's] household,* and to purify you with [extensive] purification. [33:33]

وَقَرْنَ فِي بُيُوتِكُنَّ وَلَا تَبَرَّجْنَ تَبَرُّجَ ٱلْجَٰهِلِيَّةِ ٱلْأُولَىٰ وَأَقِمْنَ ٱلصَّلَوٰةَ وَءَاتِينَ ٱلزَّكَوٰةَ وَأَطِعْنَ ٱللَّهَ وَرَسُولَهُۥٓ إِنَّمَا يُرِيدُ ٱللَّهُ لِيُذْهِبَ عَنكُمُ ٱلرِّجْسَ أَهْلَ ٱلْبَيْتِ وَيُطَهِّرَكُمْ تَطْهِيرًا ۝

Al-Qatadah states that al-Husain was born six years and five and half months after the Hijrah (Prophet's migration). Al-Husain was killed on a Friday on the day of Ashoora' (the 10th day of the Islamic month of Muharram) in the sixty-first year, aged 54 years and six and a half months (May Allah be pleased with him).

It is said that the Messenger of Allah (Peace and Blessings of Allah be upon him) made dua (prayer) for him to be blessed with wisdom and experience. The Prophet rubbed his blessed saliva in his mouth while supplicating for him. And it was the Prophet (Peace and Blessings of Allah be Upon Him) who named him Husain. Anas is reported to have said: "I was with Ibn Ziyad when the head of al-Husain was brought to him. Ibn Ziyad started poking at the nose and mouth of al-Husain with a stick, upon which he made some reference to his handsome features.

So I said to him: "Al-Husain resembled the Prophet (Peace and Blessings of Allah be upon him) more than the others did."

Al-Husain lived most of his young life with the Messenger of Allah (Peace and Blessings of Allah be Upon Him) and despite being very young, he was a Companion whom the Prophet (Peace and Blessings of Allah be upon him) was pleased with until his death. After that, as-Siddeeq (i.e., Abu Bakr) treated him the same way by honoring and respecting him, as did 'Umar and 'Uthman. He was a companion of his father, he would narrate Ahadeeth on his authority, and he participated in all the invasions with him, specifically in the battles of al-Jamal and Siffeen. As a result, when his brother gave up the caliphate and sought to reconcile matters with Mu'awiyah, al-Husain was greatly troubled and urged his brother to go to war with the people of ash-Sham. In spite of his reluctance, however, once Mu'awiyah assumed the caliphate, al-Husain would frequently visit Mu'awiyah with his brother and he would show them great hospitality and honor in return.

Following al-Hasan's death, al-Husain would travel to see Mu'awiyah every year, who would generously present him with kind gestures and treat him with great esteem. He was in the army that invaded al-Qustanteeniyyah (Constantinople) under the commandership of Mu'awiyah's son, Yazeed, in the fifty-first year.

When Mu'awiyah died in the sixtieth year and allegiance was pledged to Yazeed, Ibn 'Abbas and Ibn 'Umar offered their pledges and therefore resolved to dispute al-Husain and Ibn az-Zubair, who had left al-Madinah and went to reside in Makkah. There, the people devoted themselves to al-Husain by visiting him frequently, sitting around him and attentively listening to what he had to say about Mu'awiyah's death and Yazeed's assumption of power. As for Ibn az-Zubair, he would remain at his place of prayer by the Ka'bah, despite the fact that delegations and military detachments had been dispatched to Makkah to capture him. Nonetheless, Allah granted him victory over them and defeated whoever else desired his death among the supporters of Yazeed, including his own brother, 'Umar, whom Ibn az-Zubair beat and imprisoned -- an act for which he later became renowned.

However, in spite of all this, he was not heralded by the people in the same manner as al-Husain, for the simple reason that al-Husain was regarded as a noble due to his relation as the son of the Prophet's daughter. Even though during that time there was nobody on the face of the earth who was superior to al-Husain, or who could even be considered equal to him, the entire "Yazidite" state opposed him. In contrast, letters and messages came frequently from al-Iraq inviting al-Husain to go to them.

As the letters began to accumulate and the messengers continued to arrive, the people of al-'Iraq increasingly urged al-Husain to go to them so that they could pledge their allegiance to him in place of Yazeed bin Mu'awiyah, since they had not yet pledged allegiance to anyone. Eventually, al-Husain decided to send his paternal cousin, Muslim bin 'Aqeel bin Abi Talib to al-Iraq to determine the nature of the matter and its credibility. Upon departing from Makkah, Muslim passed through al-Madinah in order to obtain two witnesses to take with him on the desolate road. In the middle of their journey, however, one of the witnesses was lost and fled, while the other one died from the harsh conditions of the desert.

In due course, Muslim arrived in al-Koofah alone, and upon his arrival he allegedly stayed with a man called Muslim bin 'Awsajah al-Asadi.

Soon enough, word spread among the people of al-Koofah that Muslim had arrived and so they went to him, pledging their allegiance to al-Husain, as well as vowing to assist him by means of their own selves and their wealth. The number of people who agreed to pledge allegiance to him numbered approximately twelve thousand, which later increased to somewhere around eighteen thousand people. Accordingly, Muslim wrote to al-Husain affirming that he should come, assuring him of the validity of their allegiance and that he would make the necessary arrangements for his arrival in the meantime. Immediately, al-Husain embarked on the journey from Makkah to al-Koofah, which then became widespread knowledge that reached even the governor of al-Koofah, an-Nu'man bin Basheer, who in turn said: "I do not wage war against whoever does not wage war against me, nor do I ambush whoever does not ambush me."

On the other hand, 'Abdullah bín Muslím bín Shu'bah al-Hadramí went to an-Nu'man and said to him: "This course of action that you are pursing, O leader, is the course of the weak and feeble." He replied: "That is because I am weak in obedience to Allah; do you want me to be one of the strong and great in disobedience to Him?"

Upon hearing of an-Nu'man's response, Yazeed gave orders for his dismissal from al-Koofah, which he abruptly decided to merge with al-Basrah under the sole governorship of 'Ubaidullah bin Ziyad. This drastic move by Yazeed was undertaken primarily for his own protection and security, and even though Yazeed hated 'Ubaidullah bin Ziyad who he originally planned to dismiss from al-Basrah, he ended up entrusting him with authority over both al-Basrah and al-Koofah, as was the Will of Allah.

Soon after, Yazeed wrote to Ibn Ziyad, saying: "When you arrive in al-Koofah, seek out Muslím bín 'Aqeel and suppress him by either killing or humiliating him."

Accordingly, Ibn Ziyad travelled from al-Basrah to al-Koofah where he resided at the royal palace. Once he had established his authority there, he then sent a slave called Ma'qil of the Banu Tameem tribe with three thousand Dirhams, destined for the city of Hims (in central Syria) so that Ma'qil could take the money to the house in which Muslim bin 'Aqeel was taking the pledges of allegiance from the people. He was to say that he had come to offer his pledge in order to gain access. On arriving there, Ma'qil offered his pledge and so was let in to see Muslim bin 'Aqeel, who subsequently kept him there for a number of days until he demonstrated his sincerity. After that, the slave left from there and returned to 'Ubaidullah and informed him of the whereabouts of the house and its occupiers.

Meanwhile, Muslim bin 'Aqeel moved to the house of Hani' bin 'Urwah al-Muradi, and then a second time to the house of Shareek bin al-A'war, one of the senior chiefs who had been informed that 'Ubaidullah was pursuing him. Upon hearing this he sent a message to Hani' saying: "Send Muslim bin 'Aqeel to me so that he may kill 'Ubaidullah in my house if he happens to come here looking for him."

Thus, he was sent to Shareek who said to Muslim: "Go and stay in the tent outside so that when 'Ubaidullah comes in, I will ask for some water to be fetched, which will be my cue to you to come in and kill him." Sure enough, 'Ubaidullah arrived at the house of Shareek and sat down on his couch, at which point Shareek shouted: "Bring me some water to drink." Reluctant to take action, Muslim backed down from killing him and as a slave girl entered the tent with a small jug for the water, she found Muslim in a nervous state and so quickly ran out.

Shareek repeated his instruction three times, at which point 'Ubaidullah quickly realized that he was being set up and signaled to his guard that they should leave immediately, which they did. It follows that Shareek said to Muslim: "What prevented you from coming in and killing him?" He said: "I heard a Hadeeth in which the Messenger (Peace and Blessings of Allah be upon him) said: 'Faith has prevented treacherous assassination. A believer does not commit treacherous assassination. ' Thus, I detested the idea of conniving to kill him in your house."

At this, Shareek said: "Even if you had killed him while sitting in the palace, nobody would have prepared him for that, but you would have settled al-Basrah's affairs. Had you killed him, you would have killed an insolent oppressor."

It had been alleged by some that 'Ubaidullah went back to the house of Shareek bin al-A'war while Muslim bin 'Aqeel was there and attempted to kill him, although Hani' did not permit them to enter his house. The chiefs subsequently took Hani' bin 'Urwah before 'Ubaidullah bin Ziyad, upon which Ubaidullah turned to the judge, Shuraih, and quoted the saying of a poet (in al-Wafir poetry)

*"I want his life and he wants my death,*

*Your friend desires that you excuse him."*

After Hani' had greeted 'Ubaidullah, he said: "O Hani'! Where is Muslim bin 'Aqeel?" Hani' replied: "I do not know." So 'Ubaidullah said: "Bring him to me." Hani' replied: "By Allah! If he were under my feet I would not lift them up."

Ubaidullah then ordered his men to draw Hani' near to him, which they did and then 'Ubaidullah struck him in the face with a spear until he gave him a head wound and a broken nose. Hani' then reached for the sword of 'Ubaidullah's guard to stab him with it but he was pushed away, at which point 'Ubaidullah said: "Allah has made your blood lawful to me because of your provocation." Then he ordered his imprisonment.

When news of this reached Muslim bin 'Aqeel, he mounted his steed while shouting the war cry: "O Mansoor! Die! "In doing so, he rallied together some forty-thousand supporters from al-Koofah, including the likes of al-Mukhtar bin Abu 'Ubaid and 'Abdullah bin Nawfal bin al-Harith, who aligned themselves to his right and his left as they advanced against 'Ubaidullah. When Muslim arrived at the palace gates he stood before it with his army, as the tribal leaders who were with 'Ubaidullah in the palace looked out from the window urging their people (who had joined Muslim) to desist, and warned and threatened them if they did not.

Following this, 'Ubaidullah went out in the company of some of the leaders and commanded the people to return to al-Koofah and desert Muslim bin 'Aqeel, which they did.

The people slowly started abandoning him, leaving him one by one until just five-hundred supporters remained, but soon even this number fell to three-hundred and then, in the end, a mere thirty men. As the Maghrib (sunset) prayer was due, Muslim went away to lead his remaining supporters in prayer, after which they were to set out in the direction of the palace gates. However, to Muslim's dismay, a further ten men withdrew, followed by a second lot of ten and then another, until he stood alone with no one to show him the way to the palace, which he was unable to find on his own.

As he came across a door, he entered and made his way down the path to find a woman, who it is said was called Taw'ah. He said to her: "I am Muslim bin 'Aqeel. These people have lied and deceived me." She replied: "Are you Muslim?"

He answered: "Yes." She said: "You may enter", as she led him into one of the rooms of her house. Her son, having seen her go in and out of the house numerous times, asked: "What is happening?" As he pleaded with her to tell him, she informed him of Muslim's presence after warning him not to tell anyone, upon which he went to lie down, not speaking to anyone until the next morning.

Ubaidullah came out from the palace in the company of the leaders and noblemen to address the people to request them to seek out Muslim bin 'Aqeel and hand him over. That morning, when the son of the old lady in whose home Muslim had stayed saw 'Abdur-Rahman bin Muhammad bin al-Ash'ath, he revealed to him that Muslim bin 'Aqeel was staying at their house. Immediately, 'Abdur-Rahman went to his father who was sitting with Ibn Ziyad and said to him: "What is it that brings you here?" He then gave him the news, at which point Ibn Ziyad said, as he prodded him with his rod: "Get up and bring him to me within the next hour."

At the same time, Ibn Ziyad sent out 'Amr bin Huraith al-Makhzoomi at the head of approximately seventy or eighty horsemen. Completely unaware that they were surrounding him, Muslim did not realize he was being attacked until they set the surrounding area of the house on fire. When they entered upon him, Muslim jumped up in bewilderment and as he went to draw his sword on them, he cut his own lips with it. As they launched rocks at him, he was able to withstand their attack and fought back remarkably, until he killed them all.

Soon after that 'Abdur-Rahman arrived and offered him security as he stretched out his hand to him and mounted him on his mule after having disarmed him of his sword. When Muslim realized he was not carrying (his sword), he began to cry as at that point his death had become apparent to him. Giving up all hope, he said: "To Allah do we belong and to Him we shall return."

Being certain of his impending death, Muslim turned to Muhammad bin al-Ash'ath and said:

"If it is possible for you to send word on my behalf to al-Husain instructing him to go back, then do so." Despite Muhammad bin al-Ash'ath complying with his request, al-Husain failed to believe the messenger even though he testified that everything he said was true.

As Muslim entered upon Ibn Ziyad, he did not offer greetings of peace, because of which al-Harasi said to him: "Do you not send peace on the Ameer (leader)?" He replied: "No. If he insists on killing me then there is no obligation on me to offer him greetings of peace, though if he does not want to kill me then I will send many salutations of peace upon him." Ibn Ziyad then approached him and said: "Allah will surely kill me if I do not kill a murderer who no one in Islam has yet killed to keep him away from the people." Muslim replied: "As for you, you have the most right in Islam to do what has not been done before. As for you, you cannot allow an evil murderer, a malicious example and an evil way that resembles the conduct of your forefathers and the ignorant to prevail." At this, Ibn Ziyad began to vilify him, Husain and 'Ali, while Muslim stood in silence, without responding or recanting.

After completing his tirade against them, Ibn Ziyad said: "I will certainly kill you." Muslim replied: "Is that so?" He said: "Yes." So Muslim asked: "Then allow me to make some requests to some of my people." Ibn Ziyad said: "Go ahead", at which point Muslim looked around at those who were sitting in his presence, amongst whom was 'Umar bin Sa'd bin Abi Waqqas.

Muslim said to him: "You and I are related therefore I require something from you that is a private matter. I have a debt in al-Koofah amounting to seven-hundred Dirhams that I want you to repay for me. Take my body from Ibn Ziyad and bury me, then seek out al-Husain, as I have written to him informing him that the people here support him and so I am certain that he will be determined to make his way here. " 'Umar then stood up and conveyed to Ibn Ziyad what had been said to him, upon which Ibn Ziyad authorized him to fulfill all of Muslim's requests.

Ibn Ziyad then ordered that Muslim bin 'Aqeel be taken up to the highest part of the palace, during which he kept extolling the greatness of Allah, saying the words "La ilaha illallah" (there is no one worthy of worship but Allah), glorifying and seeking the forgiveness of Allah, and sending prayers and peace upon the Angels of Allah. Subsequently, Muslim was executed by beheading, supposedly at the hands of Bukair bin Humran who brutally threw his head followed by his body down to the lowest part of the palace. Hani' bin 'Urwah al-Madhhiji was also charged with the same sentence and was therefore beheaded publicly in the Sooq ul-Ghanam (Market of Sheep). Both their heads were sent to Yazeed bin Mu'awiyah in ash-Sham accompanied with a letter to explain what had happened. Muslim bin 'Aqeel departed from al-Koofah on a Tuesday, eight days past of Dhul-Hijjah, while others state it happened on a Wednesday, nine days past of Dhul-Hijjah, coinciding with the Day of 'Arafat Dhul Hijjah; the day pilgrims gather in the plains of Arafat during the rites of Hajj) of the sixtieth year. This occurred just one day after al-Husain had left Makkah for al-'Iraq, having left al-Madinah to go to Makkah on Sunday, two nights before the end of the month of Rajab of the sixtieth year. He entered

Makkah on a Friday night, three days past Sha'ban, where he spent the rest of the month as well as that of Ramadan, Shawwal and Dhul-Qa'dah. Following this, he left Makkah eight days into the month of Dhul-Hijjah on Tuesday, specifically on the Day of Tarwiyah ('watering'; Dhul Hijjah, one of the days marking the rites of Hajj).

## A Description of al-Husain's Departure and an Account of What Later Happened to Him

When al-Husain received a series of letters from the people of al-'Iraq, he began to correspond with them frequently until he finally resolved to leave Makkah during the days of Tarwiyah (watering) in order to go to them. The people of Makkah, however, were concerned for his safety and cautioned him against going, pleading with him to stay in Makkah.

Ibn 'Abbas is reported to have said: "Al-Husain ibn 'Ali sought my counsel concerning his departure, so I said to him: 'If it were not for people despising me for it, I would have held you by your head and stopped you from leaving. ' His reply to me was: 'To be killed in such and such a place is more beloved to me than being killed in Makkah. ' It was his response to what I had said that gave me some solace after that. "

Ibn 'Abbas then left as Ibn Zubair entered and said to him: "I do not know why you want to leave us for that nation when we are the sons of the Muhajireen (Emigrants) and they are without any leading personalities. Tell me, what is it that you want to do exactly?" Al-Husain said: "By Allah! I have been questioning myself over going to al-Koofah since my band of supporters started writing to me, and so I decided to honor them with my visit after performing Istikharah (guidance prayer; seeking the counsel of Allah through prayer and supplication)."

Ibn Zubair replied: "If I had a band of supporters like yours, I would not want to give them such an honor." Later that evening, or the following day, Ibn Abbas went to see al-Husain once again and added: "O my paternal cousin! I want to have patience although I cannot endure it, for I certainly fear your death. Verily, the people of al-Iraq are a treacherous nation, therefore do not be deceived by them. Stay in this country until the people of al-'Iraq have expelled their enemies, then go to them; or if not, go to Yemen, as they too have a citadel and a nation, and they will not refuse to support you.

Keep your distance from the people of al-'Iraq, just write to them and let them know of your requests, as I believe if you do this then you will get what you want." Al-Husain answered: "O my cousin! By Allah, I know that you are a compassionate and great advisor, however, I am determined to go. " Ibn 'Abbas said to him: "If it is necessary that you go then do not take your children and wives, as by Allah, I fear that you will be killed like 'Uthman, while his wives and children were watching him. Ibn 'Abbas then asked: "Have you decided to appoint Ibn az-Zubair as your successor over al-Hijaz? For by Him besides Whom there is no deity worthy of worship, if I knew that you were going to do that I would have taken you by your hair and forelock and made sure we concurred that the people would obey me and that you put me in charge. "

Once Ibn 'Abbas left al-Husain, he encountered Ibn az-Zubair to whom he said: "Your appointment has been determined, O Ibn az-Zubair", who said:

*"What is a skylark in a flourishing place?*

*You are free and safe to lay eggs and tweet;*

*Peck as you wish and wherever you wish. "*

Ibn 'Umar stated that he was in Makkah when he heard that al-Husain bin 'Ali had left for al-'Iraq and so he went to catch up with him, which he did after having travelled for three whole nights. At that point, he said to him: "Where do you want to go?" Carrying some scrolls and letters, al-Husain said: "Al-'Iraq. These are their scrolls and letters." So Ibn 'Umar said: "Do not go to them", but al-Husain refused. Ibn 'Umar then said: "I will narrate a Hadeeth to you. Once, Jibreel came to the Prophet (Peace and Blessings of Allah be upon him) and made him choose between the world and the Hereafter, so he chose the Hereafter and to never return to the world. You are a part of the Messenger of Allah (Peace and Blessings of Allah be upon him) and, by Allah, no one has ever neglected or resisted you and Allah has never dissuaded anyone from you (the family of the Prophet) except for that which was better for you."

Despite having said this, al-Husain still refused to go back. Ibn 'Umar said that after that, he hugged him and started to cry, saying: "I call on Allah to protect you from death."

Bishr bin Ghalib is reported to have said that Ibn az-Zubair said to al-Husain: "Where do you want to go, to a nation who murdered your father and defamed your brother?" So he said: "To be killed in such and such a place is more beloved to me than to be deemed unlawful (i.e. in Makkah)."

Abu Sa'eed al-Khudri stated: "I was overwhelmed by al-Husain leaving so I said to him: 'Fear Allah for yourself, hold fast to your house (i.e. the family of the Prophet (Peace and Blessings of Allah be upon him)) and do not abandon your leadership.'"

Jabir bin 'Abdullah said: "When I spoke to al-Husain, I said to him: 'Fear Allah and do not allow the people to fight one another, for by Allah, you will not be commended for what you seek to do', so he renounced me."

Amrah bint Abdur-Rahman wrote to al-Husain out of concern for what he intended to do, enjoining him to be obedient and to stick by his community, informing him that if he were to go ahead then this would lead to his destruction.

She said: "I witnessed that 'A'ishah (May Allah be pleased with her) said that she heard the Messenger of Allah (Peace and Blessings of Allah be upon him) say: 'Al-Husain will be killed in the land of Babel.'" When he read the letter, he said: "My destruction is therefore inevitable and will happen."

Another account states that before al-Husain set off to al-Madinah, those people from the Banu Abdul-Muttalib tribe who were to accompany him on his journey were sent ahead of him. They numbered nineteen men, women and children from his siblings, offspring and wives. Muhammad, the son of al-Hanafiyyah, followed them after meeting al-Husain in Makkah and warned him that he should not travel on that particular day; however, al-Husain refused to take his advice.

The people of al-'Iraq sent to al-Husain messengers and letters of invitation, upon which he, his family and sixty of his associates from al-Koofah set out to go to them. This took place on a Monday on the tenth day of Dhul-Hijjah. It follows that Marwan wrote to Ibn Ziyad stating:

"Al-Husain bin 'Ali is on his way to you. He is al-Husain, the son of Fatimah, daughter of Messenger of Allah (Peace and Blessings of Allah be upon him) and, by Allah, He has not given anyone else more beloved to us than al-Husain. Be sure to prepare yourself to say and do the right thing, do not let the public forget him, and do not let him be the last to be mentioned or greeted."

Abdullah bin Sulaim al-Asadi and al-Madhri bin al-Mushma'ill al-Asadi are reported to have said: "Al-Husain circumambulated the House (Ka'bah), performed the seven circuits between as-Safa and al-Marwah (two hills located in the Masjid al-Haram, the Holy Sanctuary in Makkah), cut his hair, completed his 'Umrah (minor Pilgrimage) and then headed for al-Koofah, while the rest of us headed towards Mina.

Abu Mikhanaf narrates in his first account that al-Farazdaq encountered al-Husain while he was on the road, whereupon he offered him greetings of peace and said: "May Allah fulfil your wishes and aspirations, just as you want them to be."

Al-Husain asked him about the affairs of the people and what was ahead of him, so he said: "The hearts of the people are with you, while their swords are with the Banu Umayyah tribe. The decree will descend from the Heavens and Allah will do what He wills." Al-Husain replied: "You have spoken the truth. The matter is with Allah, before and after, He does what He wills and everyday our Lord is engaged in some affair."

Twenty-seven days before his execution, Muslim had written to al-Husain stating that a leader should not tell a lie to his people, that the people of al-Koofah were with him and that he should set out upon reading his letter, which he closed by offering him salutations of peace. Qais bin Mus-hir as-Saidawi subsequently came forth with al-Husain's letter, whereupon he ascended the pulpit and began to praise and glorify Allah. He then said: "O people! Indeed, this is al-Husain bin 'Ali, the best of all Allah's creation. He is the son of Fatimah, the daughter of the Messenger of Allah (Peace and Blessings of Allah be upon him), and I am his messenger to you."

He then went on to say that al-Husain had departed from the center of Dhur-Rummah in al-Hijaz, and that they should respond and listen to him and obey him. He then cursed 'Ubaidullah bin Ziyad and his father and sought forgiveness for 'Ali and al-Hasan. Following his address to the people, Ibn Ziyad ordered him to be taken to the top of the palace tower and beheaded. Other accounts state that he ordered his bones to be broken and to be left for dead. Afterwards, 'Abdul-Malik bin 'Umair al-Lakhmi stood over him and slit his throat, about which he said: "I wanted to relieve him from suffering any pain."

Abdullah bin Sulaim al-Asadi and al-Madhri bin al-Mushma'ill al-Asadi are reported to have said: "Once we had completed our Hajj Pilgrimage, we had no other task to complete except to meet al-Husain and so we went to see him. Al-Husain had passed by a man from Banu Asad tribe whom he spoke to and asked questions before his departure. We later saw that man and so we started to ask him about the people, to which he said: 'By Allah! I did not leave al-Koofah until Muslim bin Aqeel and Hani' bin Urwah had been executed, prior which I saw them running through the market.

When we met with al-Husain, we informed him of what the man had told us and so he remarked: 'To Allah we belong and to Him we shall return.'" Some of al-Husain's companions turned to him and said: "By Allah! You are not like Muslim bin 'Aqeel, for if you had gone to al-Koofah the people would have got to you sooner."

Thus, al-Husain continued on his journey until he reached Zarood (a village not far from Samarqand) where received news of the death of the messenger he had sent with his letter to the people of al-Koofah after he had set out from Makkah and arrived in Hajir. Husain proclaimed:

"Our followers have disgraced us! Therefore whoever among you wishes to go back then you may do so and there will be no blame on the one who does so, as we cannot offer him protection." At that point, the people began to disperse in all directions until only those companions who had set out with him from Makkah remained.

It follows that just before daybreak, he ordered two of his servant boys to fetch him some water to drink and to fill up some to take with him on his journey, after which he embarked on his way until he came to the center of al-'Aqabah where he stationed himself.

Yazeed ar-Rishk narrated that someone who reported to have seen al-Husain said: "I saw a tent pitched in the ground within the waterless desert, so I said: 'To whom does this belong?' They said: 'This belongs to al-Husain.' Then I went to the tent where I found a Shaikh (old man) reciting the Qur'an with tears flowing down his cheeks and beard. I said: 'By my father and mother! O son of the daughter of the Messenger of Allah (Peace and Blessings of Allah be upon him)! What brings you to stay in this country and within this waterless desert in which no life exists?' He replied: 'These are the letters that the people of al-Koofah sent to me and it seems that I will not see them without being killed. However, if they choose to do that then they will not invoke the sanctity of Allah except that it will be violated, as Allah will burden them with a ruler who will degrade and humiliate them until they become the scum of the Ummah (nation).'"

It is also narrated that al-Husain said: "By Allah! They do not invite me other than to suck out the blood from inside me, and if they do this, Allah will certainly afflict them with a ruler who will make them the lowest scum of the Ummah." He was killed in Neenawa (Nineveh) on the day of 'AShoora (the tenth day of the first Islamic holy month of Muharram) in the sixty-first year. Shihab bin Khirash narrated on the authority of a man from his community who said: "I was assigned to the army that had been dispatched by Ibn Ziyad to fight against al-Husain. We were four-thousand strong and it was as we engaged in battle that I first encountered al-Husain for myself. He had black hair and a black beard, and I said to him: 'Peace be upon you, O Abu 'Abdullah!' He said: 'Peace be upon you too' in a kind of nasal tone, then he said: 'Some mysterious people from amongst you have been with us since last night', i.e. he was referring to thieves."

Abu Ma'shar reported on the authority of some of his elders that when al-Husain arrived in Karbala', he said: "What is the name of this land?" They replied: "Karbala.'" He said: "'Karb' (suffering) and 'bala' (affliction).'"

Ubaidullah bin Ziyad sent out 'Umar bin Sa'd against al-Husain who said to him: "O 'Umar! Choose one of three options: either that you leave and go back to wherever you came from; or if you refuse to do that then take me to Ibn Ziyad and put my hand in his and let him judge me according to what he sees; or if you refuse to do either of these things, then you leave me no choice but to fight you until my death." At that point, 'Umar sent Shamir bin Dhul-Jawshan to Ibn Ziyad with the message, who then sent him back with his reply, saying: "There is no option other than for you to relinquish your rule." Al-Husain remarked: "By Allah, I am not prepared to do that."

Consequently, Umar proceeded towards him with Shamir bin Dhul-Jawshan, to whom Ibn Ziyad had said: "Let 'Umar proceed to fight al-Husain, but if al-Husain kills him then you take his place and then you will be entrusted with leadership." 'Umar was backed by almost thirty men comprising the prominent people of al-Koofah. At that point, al-Husain's associates said to them: "The son of the daughter of the Prophet (Peace and Blessings of Allah be upon him) has proposed three options to you, therefore will you not agree to any of them?"

For this reason they decided to switch sides to fight alongside al-Husain. Husain is reported to have said: "I was informed by Sa'd bin 'Ubaidah about the killing of al-Husain who said to me: 'I saw al-Husain wearing a loose Jubbah (long outer garment). A man, supposedly 'Amr bin Khalid at-Tuhawi, shot an arrow at him and as I looked to see where the arrow had struck, I saw that it was caught in al-Husain's Jubbah.'"

When al-Husain's head was brought to Ibn Ziyad it was placed between his hands, after which he started to prod at his nose with a stick and say: "Abu 'Abdullah, certainly you had hair that was a mixture of black and grey." It is said that when al-Husain's wives, children and family were brought to Ibn Ziyad, he said: "The best thing that al-Husain did was to order them to reside in an isolated place to where he would send them their means of livelihood to pay for their expenses and clothing." The servant of Mu'awiyah bin Abu Sufyan is reported to have said: "When Yazeed came with al-Husain's head and placed it in his hands, I saw Yazeed crying and he said:

If there had been any relationship between Ibn Ziyad and al-Husain then he would not have done this (referring to Ibn Ziyad).'" Also in this year, 'Amr bin Sa'eed bin al-'As led the people on the Hajj Pilgrimage.

## Upon Entering the Sixty-First Year

This year notably commenced with al-Husain bin 'Ali's journey to al-Koofah, where he was later killed on the day of 'AShoora' (the tenth day of the holy month of Muharram) also in this year.

## A Description of His Murder

Based on the Accounts of the Communities Involved in this Affair, Not According to the Claims of those Bias Partisans who Lie and Make False Accusations Abdullah bin Sulaim al-Asadi and al-Madhri bin al-Mushma'ill al-Asadi are reported to have said: "When al-Husain was due to embark on his journey, he told two of his servants just before dawn to fetch him some water to drink and to take with him for the road. They then set off at daybreak."

Al-Husain took the road left until he decided to halt at his desired location where he gave orders for his tent to be pitched, and it was pitched accordingly. Soon after, a thousand horsemen led by al-Hurr bin Yazeed at-Tameemi, who formed the vanguard of Ibn Ziyad's army, arrived at al-Husain's location and stood facing him on the horizon. Al-Husain therefore ordered his companions to quench their thirst and water their horses, including the horses of their enemies.

When the time for the Zuhr (noon) prayer commenced, al-Husain emerged from his tent wearing an Izar (lower body wrap-like garment), Rida' (upper body wrap-like garment) and sandals to deliver a sermon to the people until the call to prayer was established. Then Husain said to al-Hurr and said: "Do you want to lead your companions in prayer?" He said: "No, I would rather you lead the prayer and we pray behind you." Thus, al-Husain offered the prayer with them and then went back into his tent. When the time for 'Asr (afternoon) prayer arrived, al-Husain came out and led the people in prayer again, after which he was brought two saddle bags full of letters, which he spread out in his hands and read a number of them. At that point, Al-Hurr said: "We are not like those people who write to you concerning a matter. In fact, we were commanded to meet you in person and to not part from you until we have taken you to 'Ubaidullah bin Ziyad. " So al-Husain said: "Death is closer to you than that." Al-Hurr therefore said to him: "I was not ordered to kill you but instead to not separate from you until I take you to Ibn Ziyad in al-Koofah. If you refuse, then you should take a road that neither leads you to al-Koofah nor takes you back to al-Madinah. Then you may write to Yazeed yourself and I will write to Ibn Ziyad, and perhaps Allah will grant me livelihood and good health for undergoing something for your sake."

Hence, al-Husain took the road left leading to al-'Adheeb and al-Qadisiyyah while al-Hurr bin Yazeed travelled alongside him as he said to him: "O Husain! I make you mindful of Allah, as I swear if you go into battle you will either kill or be killed. " So al-Husain said: "So it is death that you fear for me? Rather, I say that which the brother of al-Aws said to his paternal cousin when he encountered him wanting to serve the Messenger of Allah (Peace and Blessings of Allah be upon him).

His cousin asked him: "Where are you going, to be killed?" He replied (in at-Taweel poetry):

> *"I will proceed; death is not shameful for a young man.*
>
> *If his intentions were truly to be a Muslim warrior,*
>
> *He compared himself with righteous men.*
>
> *And so detached himself from fear as he lived and led the way."*

When al-Hurr heard that from him, he decided to desist and led his associates in the direction of 'Udhaibul-Hijanat. There, they encountered 4 individuals who had arrived from al-Koofah having believed al-Husain based on the conviction of a man known as at-Tirimmah bin 'Adiyy, who had proclaimed aloud while riding his horse (in ar-Rajaz poetic meter):

> *"O... My she-camel! Do not be afraid of my suppression*
>
> *And be prepared before the dawn*
>
> *To carry the best travelers on the best journey*
>
> *For you will be oriented towards beneficent descent,*
>
> *The noble, glorious and tolerant.*
>
> *God has brought him to execute the optimal deed*
>
> *May God protect him forever and ever."*

Upon hearing this, al-Hurr had wanted to come between them and al-Husain but al-Husain prevented him from doing so. The group of four then approached al-Husain who said to them: "Tell me about the people you have come from." So Mujammi' bin 'Abdullah al-A'idhi, one of the four men, said: "As for the distinguished amongst them, they are the most mindful of you. With regard to the rest of the people, their hearts go out to you and their swords will tomorrow be a source of fame for you."

Following this, at-Tirimmah bin 'Adiyy said to al-Husain: "Look at what you have. I do not see that you have anyone except this insignificant small band of supporters and I see those people who agree with you being suited to those who are with you. Al-Koofah is replete with horses and armies, therefore how do you think you will fare with them? I implore by Allah that if it is possible for you to not go to them then do not, and if you want to stay in a land which Allah has made impenetrable until you have decided then come with me and I will take you to our impassable mountains."

Al-Husain said to him: "May Allah reward you", however he did not take recourse to his advice and so at-Tirimmah bid him farewell and al-Husain departed. When it was night, he ordered his two servant boys to quench their thirst and then once he had relaxed, he set off while he was still drowsy and so he fell asleep. When he woke up, he said: "To Allah we belong and to Him we shall return. All praise belongs to Allah, the Lord of the Worlds."

He took the left road in his journey until he came to Neenawa (Nineveh) where a riding man came towards al-Koofah with a bow on his shoulder. The man greeted al-Hurr bin Yazeed, although he did not greet al-Husain, and then presented al-Hurr with a letter from Ibn Ziyad which stated that he should divert al-Husain on his journey to al-'Iraq, to a town in which there was no fortress until Ibn Ziyad's associates and soldiers arrived. This took place on a Thursday on the second day of al-Muharram of the sixty-first year. The following day, 'Umar bin Sa'd bin Abi Waqqas advanced with an army of four thousand men which Ibn Ziyad had previously assembled in ad-Dailam in the outskirts of al-Koofah. Ibn Ziyad had issued the instructions to them:

"Advance towards al-Husain and once you have annihilated him then station yourselves in ad-Dailam." At that point, 'Umar bin Sa'd attempted to submit his resignation to Ibn Ziyad, to which Ibn Ziyad responded: "If you wish, you may be excused and discharged from your post in this land that has raised you." He therefore said: "I need to contemplate on the matter some more." 'Umar's nephew, Hamzah bin al-Mugheerah bin Shu'bah, later advised him: "Be wary of going to al-Husain as you may disobey your Lord and sever your bonds of kinship. But, by Allah, renouncing the entire authority of the land is better for you than to meet Allah with al-Husain's blood on your hands. " So he said: "Indeed, I will do that if Allah wills." Subsequent to that, 'Ubaidullah bin Ziyad warned and threatened him with dismissal and death, and this was the reason he was compelled to advance against al-Husain.

To begin with, 'Umar bin Sa'd's associates denied water to al-Husain associates, a strategy that forced al-Husain to propose a meeting with 'Umar bin Sa'd between the two armies.

Thus, they both turned up with approximately twenty horsemen on each side and spoke for a long time until part of the night had passed, while nobody else knew what had been said. 'Umar then wrote to 'Ubaidullah regarding the meeting, about which he said: "Yes, I accept." At that point, ash-Shamir bin Dhul-Jawshan stood up and protested: "No, by Allah! He and his associates seek to seize your office of power." 'Ubaidullah therefore delegated ash-Shamir bin Dhul-Jawshan to the battlefield while saying to him: "Go and if al-Husain and his associates have come to claim my authority then command 'Umar bin Sa'd to battle against them and if he hesitates then decapitate him. If you do that then you will be made the commander of the people."

When ash-Shamir bin Dhul-Jawshan presented 'Umar bin Sa'd with 'Ubaidullah bin Ziyad's letter, 'Umar said: "May Allah do away with your home and defile what you came here for. By Allah! I believe that you dissuaded 'Ubaidullah bin Ziyad from the three options al-Husain requested you to propose to him." Following this, 'Umar bin Sa'd shouted to his army: "O horsemen of Allah, gallop and rejoice! Ride and advance towards them after Salat ul-'Asr (afternoon prayer) on this day of ours!"

Meanwhile, al-Husain was sitting in front of his tent, reclining with his sword clutched in his hands. He had just started to doze off when his sister, Zainab, heard the shouting and so she hastened to wake him up. Once he became fully alert, he said: "I saw the Messenger of Allah (Peace and Blessings of Allah be upon him) in my dream and he said to me: 'You are coming to us. ' Upon hearing this, Zainab struck her face in lamentation and said: "Woe to us!" He said: "There is no woe to you, O sister! Be at ease, the Most Merciful has compassion on you. " His brother, al-'Abbas bin 'Ali, then came to him and said: "O brother! The people have come for you. " He said: "Go and find out what you can from them." So he went in the company of approximately twenty horsemen and said: "What do you want?" They said: "We have come by the order of the Ameer. Either you acknowledge his authority or we will wage war against you. " So he said: "Retreat so that I may go to Abu 'Abdullah and inform him about this." When al-'Abbas returned, al-Husain said to him: "Go back and deter them this evening so that we might pray, seek forgiveness and supplicate to our Lord tonight, for Allah knows that I love to pray to Him, recite His Book, seek His forgiveness and supplicate to Him. "

Hence, al-Husain spent the first part of the night bequeathing his will to his family and delivering a sermon to his companions. He then praised and glorified Allah and sent the most eloquently articulated prayers on the Prophet (Peace and Blessings of Allah be upon him), following which he said to his companions: "Whoever would like to return to his family on this night of his then he has my permission, for these people certainly want me."

They said in response: "Then the people will say that we abandoned our Shaikh (religious leader; elder), our master and the tribe of our great paternal uncles! We did not shoot arrows with them nor did we thrust spears with them nor did we strike swords with them seeking the life of this world, so no, by Allah, we will not leave. On the contrary, we will assist you with our own selves, our wealth and our families, and we will fight with you until we return your rightful place to you. May Allah make living shameful and ugly once you are gone."

Ali bin al-Husain, "Zainul-'Abideen", is reported to have said: "I was one of those sitting down on the evening before my father was killed. As my paternal aunt, Zainab, was giving me medical treatment, my father and his companions withdrew into his tent all of a sudden. Huwayy, Abu Dharr al-Ghifari's servant, was in my father's presence as he mended and tended to his sword, when my father said:

> *"As time proceeds you are not befriended.*
>
> *How many friends, in the morning and afternoon,*
>
> *Over those who pursue you, do you really have?*
>
> *Time is not satisfied with alternatives.*
>
> *Affairs are nothing but complicated.*
>
> *All beings are to traverse this path."*

He repeated himself two or three times until I memorized it myself and understood what he wanted. The tears choked me whenever I repeated them and so I remained silent. I knew that some affliction was going to befall us and as for my aunt, she was overcome by sorrow until she could not bear it anymore, then she said:

'He bereaves me by his death and deprives me of life today. Let my father and mother be sacrificed for you, O Abu Abdullah! Have you put your life at risk?' She then slapped her face in lamentation, tore the front of her garment as a sign of mourning and fell to the floor. Al-Husain therefore went up to her, poured water on her face and said: 'O sister! Fear Allah, be patient and console yourself with the solace of Allah. 'He then forbade her from doing anything like that after his death. "

Once 'Umar bin Sa'd had finished praying as-Subh (the morning prayer) with his companions on the Friday --while others maintain it was on Saturday --on the day of 'AShoora' (the tenth day of Muharram), he got up and prepared for battle. At the same time, al-Husayn prayed with his companions, all together constituting thirty-two horsemen and forty foot-soldiers, who he subsequently organized into rows after they had set up their military base out of sight, as did 'Umar and his army. In addition, al-Husain ordered that his men dig a trench behind their base, toss firewood, timber and cane into it and then set it on fire to obstruct access to their base from behind; and these were the settings of this battle.

Furthermore, al-Husain avoided entering the tent that had been pitched for him, except when he went in to wash from time to time, but he otherwise stayed clear of falling into the trap of being caught in there. He would also enter to scent himself with Misk (musk) quite frequently and others would do so after him.

It follows that al-Husain mounted his horse, took up a Mus-haf (Arabic copy of the Qur'an), in his hands and then approached the people with it raised high, calling: "O Allah! You are my trust during agonizing times and my hope during every hardship. " He then said: "O people! Carry me off and return me to my asylum in the ground! "They said: "What prevents you from conceding to the authority of your paternal uncle's tribe?" He replied: "May God grant me refuge from degrading myself to them or endorsing the avowal of a slave. Worshippers of Allah: "Moosa (Moses) said (what means): ['Verily, I seek refuge in my Lord and your Lord from every arrogant person who believes not in the Day of Reckoning! '"] [Ghafir, 40:27].

وَقَالَ مُوسَىٰٓ إِنِّى عُذۡتُ بِرَبِّى وَرَبِّكُم مِّن كُلِّ مُتَكَبِّرٍ لَّا يُؤۡمِنُ بِيَوۡمِ ٱلۡحِسَابِ ۝

His riding camel was then made to kneel down, after which 'Uqbah bin Sim'an ordered it to be strung up by the neck.

At that point, 'Umar bin Sa'd advanced with his bow and as he shot his arrow, he proclaimed: "Bear witness that I was first to shoot at the people." Yasar, the servant of Ziyad, and Salim, the servant of 'Ubaidullah, then went out and shouted: "Who will meet in combat?" Upon obtaining al-Husain's permission, 'Ubaidullah bin 'Umairal-Kalbi then stepped forward and first killed Yasar followed by Salim, who managed to strike 'Ubaidullah a blow to the left hand that caused his fingers to fly off. That day, the two sides continued to contest against each other until al-Husain's companions beat the opposition and emerged victorious, primarily due to the strength of their archers and because they fought heroically with no defense other than their swords.

Next, Shamir bin Dhul-Jawshan led the left-wing of his army defended by an immense cavalry force towards al-Husain; the army successfully engaged in battle without Shamir's intervention. Following this, however, Shamir bin Dhul-Jawshan (may Allah disgrace him) went to the tent of al-Husain and said: "Bring me a torch so that I may blaze whoever dwells herein."

At that instant, the women began to scream and came running out and so al-Husayn retorted: "You want to burn my family, so may Allah burn you in the Hellfire!"

The time for az-Zuhr (afternoon) prayer had come in and so al-Husain said: "Order them then refrain from battle until we pray." A man from among the people of al-Koofah said: "It will not be accepted from you anyway." So Habeeb bin Muzahhir shouted back: "Woe unto you! Are your prayers accepted and not those of the family of the Messenger (Peace and Blessings of Allah be upon him)?!" Infuriated, he said, "Will your prayers be accepted and will not the prayer be accepted from the family of Yasir?" He then attacked Habeeb so aggressively that he was killed amidst the fighting (May Allah have mercy upon them), after which his head was carried off to Ibn Ziyad. Al-Husain then led his companions in offering the Salat ul-khawf (optional prayer of fear) before they commenced a brutal battle in which al-Husain's valiant companions went to magnificent lengths to defend him. As Shamir launched an attack on al-Husain's companions, he shouted:

> *"Leave God's enemies, leave Shamir*
> *Who strikes them with his sword without fleeing the battlefield."*

The chief member of the Banu Abi Talib tribe from al-Husain's family was his eldest son, 'Ali bin al-Husain bin 'Ali, whose mother was Laila bint Abu Murrah bin 'Urwah bin Mas'ood ath-Thaqafi. He was fatally stabbed by Murrah bin Munqidh bin an-Nu'man al-'Abdi because he tried to shield his father from being targeted, which caused 'Ali bin al-Husain to say:

> *"I am Ali bin al-Husain bin 'Ali,*
> *We and Allah's House are the closest to the Prophet.*
> *I swear by Allah that the son of deception will not govern us*
> *You shall see how I will guard my father today."*

Once he had been stabbed by Murrah, his men surrounded him and began to cut him into pieces with their swords. Al-Husain invoked: "May Allah kill the people who killed you my son!

They challenge Allah in their violation of His injunctions! May ruin befall the world after you go! "Following his murder, 'Abdullah bin Muslim bin 'Aqeel, 'Awn and Muhammad, the sons of 'Abdullah bin Ja'far, were also killed. Al-Husain remained alone for a whole day with no one approaching him as no one not wanted to be charged with his murder, until a man from the Banu Badda' tribe, who it is said was Malik bin an-Nusair, came to him and struck him on the head with his sword causing it to bleed. He was wearing a cloak, which he tore to bandage his wounded head, although his band quickly filled with blood. So al-Husain said to him: "May you not eat nor drink therein (in Paradise) but may it be that Allah impounds you amidst the Zalimeen (oppressors; wrongdoers)."

As al-Husain's thirst intensified, he desperately tried to obtain some water from the River Euphrates to drink but to no avail. Soon afterwards, a man, supposedly Husain bin Numair, shot an arrow that struck al-Husain in his throat, although it did not kill him. Holding his neck to prevent the blood from gushing out of his it, he then raised his bloody hands to the sky and supplicated:

"O Allah! Give them their retribution many times over, kill them wherever they may be and do not leave a single one of them on the earth!" He continued to supplicate in this manner.

Nobody else stepped forward to execute al-Husain's murder and so Shamir bin Dhul-Jawshan shouted: "Proceed! What are you waiting for? Do you want them to kill you and bereave your mothers of their sons?" Immediately, his men raced towards al-Husain and began to attack him from all angles.

The man who actually stabbed al-Husain with a spear and caused him to fall to the ground was called Sinan bin Anas bin 'Amr an-Nakha'i, who then dismounted his horse, slit al-Husain's throat and pierced him through the head, which he then severed and handed over to Khawali bin Yazeed. On the other hand, some sources indicate that was Shamir bin Dhul-Jawshan himself who murdered al-Husain. They said that Sinan bin Anas went up to the entrance of 'Umar bin Sa'd's tent and shouted at the top of his voice:

> *"Overload my mount with silver and gold*
> *For it was I who killed the masked king*
> *Who was the best fathered and mothered amongst the people*
> *And who possessed the best ancestry and lineage of all."*

Umar bin Sa'd shouted: "Enter", and when Sinan bin Anas went in, Umar flogged him with a whip and said: "Woe unto you, you crazy man! By Allah, if Ibn Ziyad were to hear what you are saying he would break your neck!"

Seventy-two of al-Husain's companions were killed in the battle and were buried by the people of al-Ghadirah (a neighboring town of al-Koofah near to Karbala') belonging to the Banu Asad tribe a day after the onslaught (may Allah bestow His mercy and blessings on them).

Al-Hasan al-Basri is reported to have said: "Sixteen other men were killed with al-Husain, all of whom were from his Ahl ul-Bait (members of his family).

It is said that 'Umar bin Sa'd commissioned ten horsemen to trample on al-Husain with their horses on the day of the battle until his body was stuck to the ground, while his head was sent with Khawali bin Yazeed al-Asbahi to Ibn Ziyad. It is said that he also took the heads of al-Husain's companions with him, which is in fact a widely recognized opinion.

The number of heads therefore amounted to seventy-two and this figure does not include all those who were killed without having their heads' severed. Once the heads were delivered to Ibn Ziyad, he sent them to Yazeed bin Mu'awiyah in ash-Sham (the Levant).

Anas is reported to have said: "'Ubaidullah bin Ziyad was brought the head of al-Husain and it was put in a tray. Ibn Ziyad started to play with it with a stick and commented on al-Husain's handsome features. So Anas said: 'Al-Husain resembled the Prophet (Peace and Blessings of Allah be upon him) more than the others did.' Anas added: 'Al-Husain's hair was dyed with Wasmah (a kind of plant used as dye).'"

Anas is also reported to have said: "When al-Husain's head was brought to 'Ubaidullah bin Ziyad, he started to prod and play with al-Husain's nose and mouth with a stick and commented on his good looks. So I said: 'By Allah! Indeed, I saw the Messenger of Allah (Peace and Blessings of Allah be upon him) kiss where you are poking your stick', which made 'Ubaidullah feel uneasy."

In another tradition, at-Tirmidhi reports that 'Umarah bin 'Umair narrated: "When the heads of Ubaidullah bin Ziyad and his companions were brought, they were stacked in the mosque at ar-Rahbah. So I went to see them and the people were saying: 'It has come, it has come!' And behold there was a snake going between the heads, until it entered the nostrils of 'Ubaidullah bin Ziyad, and it remained there momentarily, then left and went until it had disappeared. The people then said again: 'It has come, it has come!' So it did that two or three times" (Dha'eef, i. e. weak narration). Qasim bin Bukhait is reported to have said: "When al-Husain's head was placed in Yazeed bin Mu'awiyah's hands, he started to play with his mouth with a stick.

He then said: "Both this (i. e. the head) and we are like what al-Husain bin al-Humam al-Murri said in his poem (in at-Taweel poetic meter):

*"Women can bring the noses of venerated men down,*

*They were impious tyrants."*

Abu Barzah al-Aslami uttered to Yazeed: "By Allah! Perhaps you should take your stick away from him, for I saw the Messenger of Allah (Peace and Blessings of Allah be upon him) kiss him there." He then went on to say: "Will the Day of Resurrection not come when Muhammad (Peace and Blessings of Allah be upon him) will be his (al-Husain's) intercessor and you will come for your intercession, O Ibn Ziyad?" He then stood up and walked away. Al-Hasan said: "When al-Husain's head was brought, Yazeed started to ridicule it with a stick, singing the following verses:

*'Sumayyah's descendants are like stones in number*

*While the daughter of the Messenger of Allah (Peace and Blessings of Allah be upon him) is barren.'*

As for the rest of al-Husain's family and wives, 'Umar bin Sa'd entrusted them to whoever would guard and protect them, after which he mounted them onto a group of riding camels and sent them off on their journey. When they passed by the battlefield on which al-Husain and his companions had fallen, the women began to cry and wail, while Zainab lamented over her brother, al-Husain, and his family. They travelled from Karbala' until they entered al-Koofah where they were received hospitably and offered provisions and clothing. Following this, they were made to travel once again but this time they were taken back to ash-Sham with Shamir bin Dhul-Jawshan and Muhaffiz bin Tha'labah al-'A'idhi from the tribe of Quraish.

As the heads and women were presented to Yazeed, he called on the women and children to come and witness the gruesome sight, as he said: "May Allah revile Ibn Marjanah! If there had been any mercy between them and him, this would not have happened to them, nor would you have been summoned for this very reason."

Yazeed then ordered an-Nu'man bin Basheer to send a trustworthy man to accompany the women and al-Husain's younger son, 'Ali bin al-Husain, on their journey to al-Madinah and to assign guards and horsemen for their protection. The women were then taken to Yazeed's Hareem (private quarters for women) situated in the house of the caliph where they were received by the women of Mu'awiyah's family who cried and grieved for al-Husain. They stayed there for a period of three days during which Yazeed would eat neither dinner nor supper except in the company of 'Ali bin al-Husain and his brother, 'Amr bin al-Husain.

Yazeed provided them with provisions by giving them a generous amount of money as well as clothing before sending them away under the protection of his ambassador to whom Yazeed said: "Write to me informing me of every move you make." He then set out with them as he took the desolate road in order to avert any interception and he continued to remain in their service until they arrived in al-Madinah.

# Chapter on Murder

Al-Husain's murder took place on a Friday on the day of 'AShoora' (tenth day of Muharram) of the sixty-first year in place known as at-Tuff in Karbala', al-'Iraq. He was aged fifty-eight or so when he died.

Abdullah bin Nujayy narrated that his father said that he was travelling with 'Ali (May Allah be pleased with him) on their way to Neenawa (Nineveh) when they saw al-Husain heading in the direction of Siffeen. 'Ali (May Allah be pleased with him) therefore shouted out to him: "Patience, Abu 'Abdullah! Patience, Abu 'Abdullah! By the banks of the Euphrates!" So I said: "What do you mean?" He said: "I entered upon the Prophet (Peace and Blessings of Allah be upon him) one day and saw that his eyes were flowing with tears, so I said: 'O Messenger of Allah! Has somebody upset you? Are your eyes bothering you?' He said: 'No. Jibreel was just with me and he told me that al-Husain will be killed by the banks of the Euphrates.' Then he asked me: 'Do you want to smell its earth?'

I replied in the affirmative and so he stretched out his hand, grabbed a handful of the dust and then gave it to me, while I could not hold back my tears."

People have exaggerated the events of the day of 'AShoora' and have accordingly fabricated a great deal of narrations based on absurd claims and allegations, none of which can be verified as true. As for narrations pertaining to the events and conflicts surrounding al-Husain's murder in the Ahadeeth, these are mostly correct. It later emerged that those who survived after killing him were either afflicted with some disease or turmoil in the world, while the majority of them lost their senses.

The Rafidah (Dissenters; Rafidites, a Shee'ah sect) in the state of the Banu Buwaih tribe within Baghdad exceeded all bounds by beating and striking themselves out of remorse on the day of 'AShoora' in addition to scattering ashes and straw in the streets and marketplaces while crying. Many of them even deny themselves water to evoke the state of thirst in which al-Husain died.

The women strike their faces with their hands out of lamentation, as they wail and beat their chests while walking barefooted through the marketplaces, along with other horrific innovations and practices. In fact, the Rafidah and people have contradicted and greatly deviated from the practices of their ancestors in ash-Sham on the day of 'AShoora.' It is reported that they used to cook grain, bathe, apply perfume and wear their finest clothes and instead celebrated that day with a feast by making a variety of dishes, thus regarding it as a day to rejoice and be happy as their way of opposing the dissenters.

Such disastrous practices have been best addressed in a narration by 'Ali bin al-Husain, on the authority of his grandfather, the Messenger of Allah (Peace and Blessings of Allah be upon him) who said: "Whoever is stricken with a calamity and when he remembers it says: 'inna lillahi wa inna ilaihi raji'oon' ('To Allah we belong and to Him we shall return'), even though it happened a long time ago, Allah will record for him a reward like that of the day it befell him." The people that killed al-Husain and harmed him are on fire in their graves to eternity.

Allah Says: *And every soul earns not [blame] except against itself, and no bearer of burdens will bear the burden of another.* [Quran 6:164]. This verse means that no person shall be held accountable for the sins of another person that he did not commit.

﴿قُلْ أَغَيْرَ ٱللَّهِ أَبْغِى رَبًّا وَهُوَ رَبُّ كُلِّ شَىْءٍ وَلَا تَكْسِبُ كُلُّ نَفْسٍ إِلَّا عَلَيْهَا وَلَا تَزِرُ وَازِرَةٌ وِزْرَ أُخْرَىٰ ثُمَّ إِلَىٰ رَبِّكُم مَّرْجِعُكُمْ فَيُنَبِّئُكُم بِمَا كُنتُمْ فِيهِ تَخْتَلِفُونَ ١٦٤﴾

As for al-Husain's grave, many people later believed that he was buried at the place of Ali's shrine in at-Tuff by the River of Karbala. It is said that the shrine was venerated on top of his grave --Allah knows best.

With regard to al-Husain's head, a popular opinion amongst historians and biographers is that Ibn Ziyad sent it to Yazeed bin Mu'awiyah, while others deny this view. I consider the first opinion to be more credible and Allah knows best.

Furthermore, there is a difference of opinion concerning the place in which his head was buried. Muhammad bin Sa'd reported that al-Husain's head was sent to 'Amr bin Sa'eed, the deputy of al-Madinah, who buried it with al-Husain's mother in al-Baqee'(a fertile patch of land in al-Madinah where other members of the Prophet's family were buried).

Ibn Abi Dunya mentions that the head was no longer in Yazeed bin Mu'awiyah's coffer when he died. It is believed that it was therefore taken from his coffer and wrapped and buried within the Bab ul-Faradees in the city of Dimashq (Damascus).

# A Chapter Mentioning Some of His Virtues

Abu Nu'aim is reported to have said: "I heard 'Abdullah bin 'Umar saying that a man from the people of al-'Iraq asked him about the blood of housefly. Ibn 'Umar said: 'Where are you from?' The man replied: 'From al-'Iraq.' Ibn 'Umar said: 'Look at that! He is asking me about the blood of a housefly while they (the people of al-'Iraq) have killed the grandson of the Prophet (Peace and Blessings of Allah be upon him). Ibn 'Umar added: 'I heard the Messenger of Allah (Peace and Blessings of Allah be upon him) saying: 'They (Hasan and Husain) are my two sweet-smelling flowers in this world.'"

Muhammad bin Abu Ya'qoob is reported to have said that a man from the people of al-'Iraq asked 'Umar about the blood of a housefly staining the clothes. Ibn 'Umar said: 'Look at that! He is asking me about the blood of a housefly while they (the people of al-'Iraq) have killed the grandson of the Prophet (Peace and Blessings of Allah be upon him).'

Abu Hurairah is reported to have said that the Messenger of Allah (Peace and Blessings of Allah be upon him) said: "The one who loves them, loves me, and who hates them, then surely he hates me." Ya'la bin Murrah reported that the Messenger of Allah (Peace and Blessings of Allah be upon him) said: "Al-Husain is from me and I am from al-Husain, therefore whoever loves Allah loves al-Husain; he is Sibt among the Asbat (from a great tribe, lineage)."

Abu Sa'eed is reported to have said that the Messenger of Allah (Peace and Blessings of Allah be upon him) said: "Al-Hasan and al-Husain are masters over the youth in Paradise except over the two sons of al-Khalah (maternal aunt), Yahya and Eesa (John and Jesus (Peace be upon them)."

Hudhaifah reported that he went to the Prophet (Peace and Blessings of Allah be upon him) to seek forgiveness for himself and his mother, about which he said: "I went to the Prophet (Peace and Blessings of Allah be upon him) and after performing the Zuhr, Asr, Maghrib and Isha prayers with him, I turned and followed him. Upon hearing my voice, the Prophet (Peace and Blessings of Allah be upon him) said: 'Who is this? Hudhaifah?' I said: 'Yes.'

He said: 'What is your need, may Allah forgive you and your mother?' He said: 'Indeed, this is an angel that never descended to the earth before tonight. He sought permission from his Lord to greet me and give me glad tidings that Fatimah is the chief of the women of Paradise, and that al-Hasan and al-Husain are the chiefs of the youth of Paradise.' So Hudhaifah said: 'I seek forgiveness for me and my mother.' He (Peace and Blessings of Allah be upon him) said: 'Allah has forgiven you, O Hudhaifah, and your mother.'"

Abu Hurairah is reported to have said: "We were praying al-Isha (the evening prayer) with the Messenger of Allah (Peace and Blessings of Allah be upon him) and whenever he prostrated, al-Hasan and al-Husain pounced on his back, and whenever he raised his head, they would wrap their arms around him from behind and pull his head back. He would put them down on the ground and when he started again they would repeat the same thing until he had completed the whole prayer. After this, he sat them on his lap and I went to sit next to him and said: 'O Messenger of Allah (Peace and Blessings of Allah be upon him)! Whenever you put them down, lightning struck.' So he said to them: 'Stay by your mother.' The lightning continued to strike until they went in."

Ali is reported to have said: "The Messenger of Allah (Peace and Blessings of Allah be upon him) came in to see me while I was sleeping. He gave al-Hasan and al-Husain something to drink and then he got up and began to milk one of our uncultivable sheep, which thereafter produced an abundant flow of milk. After he had finished, another one came to him, however the Prophet (Peace and Blessings of Allah be upon him) pushed it aside.

Fatimah then said: 'O Messenger of Allah! It is as if they love you.' He said: 'No, it is because it quenched its thirst in front of the other. 'Then he said: 'Verily, me, you, these two (al-Hasan and al-Husain) and the one who is asleep will all be in one place on the Day of Resurrection.'"

Sulaiman bin al-Haitham have said: "Al-Husain bin 'Ali was circumambulating the House (Ka'bah) and he wanted to overtake the people but there was no space to do so. As al-Farazdaq bin Ghalib was looking at him, a man said to him: 'O Abu Firas! Who is that?' So al-Farazdaq replied (in al-Baseet poetic meter):

*"The gravity of his tread is realized by the valley*

*And he is known by the dwelling, domicile and sacred places.*

*This is the son of the best of all Allah's worshippers.*

*This is the pious, pure and chaste soul.*

*The stone (al-Hateem) would touch his palm*

*Out of gratitude when he would go to greet it."*

It is well known that al-Farazdaq would call al-Husain "'Alí bin al-Husain ('Alí, the son of al-Husain')" in jest, and not the son of his father due to the fact that he resembled him so much.

## Some Poetry Eulogizing Al-Husain

According to 'Abdullah bin Ibraheem, one poet to have eulogized al-Husain bin 'Ali bin Abu Talib (May Allah be pleased with them) in his poems was Abu Bakr bin Kamil. He wrote:

*"Sing about the Creator's creation,*

*So that you may discern the liar and the honest one;*

*Ask the Most-Gracious for His grace,*

*None other than the Lord grants sustenance.*

*Who thinks that people provide livelihood? Does one not trust the Most-Gracious?*

*Or does he think that his money is of benefit to him?*

*If so, you are surely mistaken."*

*According to al-A'mash, al-Husain bin 'Ali once said:*

*"The more money its possessors have*

*The more their worries increase.*

*We have fathomed you, O embittering life!*

*O dwelling of all mortals and ephemeral beings!*

*An ascetic would not be serene*

*If he were burdened with offspring."*

Az-Zubair bin Bakkar recited poetry about al-Husain's wife, ar-Rabab bint Unaif, while others say she was the daughter of Imra'ul-Qais bin 'Adiyy bin Aws al-Kalbi. She was the mother of al-Husain's daughter, Sukainah bint al-Husain. He said:

> "By your life! I love the house
>
> Where Sukainah and Rabab dwell.
>
> I love them and on them I am willing to spend my wealth
>
> So that my Admonisher will not have reason to blame me.
>
> And even if they blame me, I will not be compelled
>
> Throughout my entire lifetime until I am entombed."

Ar-Rabab's father embraced Islam at the hands of 'Umar bin al-Khattab, after which 'Umar made him chief of his people. Once 'Umar had left, 'Ali bin Abi Talib approached him to offer either al-Hasan or al-Husain's hand in marriage to any of his daughters.

Thus, al-Hasan married his daughter Salma and al-Husain married his other daughter, ar-Rabab, while 'Ali himself married his third daughter, al-Muhayyah bint Imra'ul-Qais all within the same hour. Al-Husain deeply loved his wife, ar-Rabab, which is evident from the way he used to recite poetry about her.

After al-Husain's death, many of the Quraish's nobles sought her hand in marriage. Her response was: "I would not have any other (grand) father-in-law after the Messenger of Allah (Peace and Blessings of Allah be upon him) nor would I ever cohabit with another man after al-Husain."

Of the many events that took place following al-Husain's murder in this year (i.e., the sixty-first year), was Yazeed bin Mu'awiyah's appointment of Salm bin Ziyad, who was just twenty-four years of age at the time, over Sijistan and Khurasan. The first task he embarked on was the appointment and selection of prominent personalities and horsemen by promoting Jihad (fighting for Allah's Cause).

He then set out with his legion on an expedition against the Turks, taking his wife, Umm Muhammad bint 'Abdullah bin 'Uthman bin Abul-'As, with him and in that way making her the first 'Arab woman to have crossed over the river into that land.

Prior to this, the Muslims had never spent the winter in that country and so Salm bin Ziyad was the first to do so. He sent al-Muhallab bin Abu Sufrah to the Turk city of Khuwarizm and laid siege to it until they agreed to reconcile matters at a sum of twenty million or so.

When news of al-Husain's murder reached az-Zubair, he stood up and began address the people, upon which he denounced the death of al-Husain and his companions and cursed those who killed him. He displayed his contempt at Yazeed bin Mu'awiyah and further incited the people to turn against the Banu Umayyah tribe, urging them to put up opposition and depose Yazeed as caliphate. In consequence to his stance, many people offered their pledge of allegiance to Ibn az-Zubair, saying: "With regard to the killing of al-Husain, not a single one of us are in disagreement with Ibn az-Zubair."

When Yazeed heard what the people were saying, he was extremely troubled by it and so it was said to him: "If you permit it, 'Amr bin Sa'eed can bring you back the head of Ibn az-Zubair or otherwise he can lay siege to him until he leaves the Haram (Holy Sanctuary in Makkah)." 'Amr was delegated to begin with, but was soon afterwards dismissed and replaced by al-Waleed bin 'Utbah in this year. Yazeed made him swear that Ibn az-Zubair would be brought to him in silver shackles.

Abu Ma'shar states that no biographer has contested the view that al-Waleed bin 'Utbah was the Ameer of the Haramain (Custodian of the Two Sanctuaries) and that he performed the Hajj Pilgrimage with the people in this year.

## Early Life

Hussain (RA) and his brother spent the early years of their lives under the shadow of the Holy Prophet (Peace be Upon Him) and their father Ali (RA) who were both exemplary men. Hence from an early age, Hussain (RA) was well aware of his duties as a Muslim and as a good human being – he used to go to congregational prayers and offer the daily prayers with devotion. The Holy Prophet trained Hussain and his brother according to the Quran and since the beginning, they were a specimen of the morals and values that Islam stands upon. Hussain used to listen to stories of wars and used to help the needy and poor just like his grandfather. Hussain's love for his religion was strong and unwavering. He saw the Holy Prophet striving for Islam and the way he talked with the people and the way he handled responsibilities, hence it is no surprise that Hussain too had a passion for Islam. Even though Husain only lived under the care of the Prophet (PBUH) and his exemplary character for only 7 years, he learned lessons that made him into the incredible Muslim and leader that he is remembered as today.

## Political endeavors

When Alí became the calíph, Hussaín was always there to assist his father and to learn from him. He learned to be brave and courageous from his father and was involved in 3 battles that were fought during the caliphate of Alí. In the battle of Jamal, Hussaín was the commanding officer of the army, his first victory on a battlefield occurred in Siffin where Hussaín and his army freed the river Euphrates. Hussaín was always very active in the arena of politics and was witness to the arbitration between Muawiyah and Alí.

Even when his brother Hassan took leadership after the death of their father Alí, Hussaín always supported his brother in all his decisions and endeavors. Like his brother, Hussaín believed that peace was a key factor for the propagation of Islam.

## Hussain – the leader

After the death of his brother, Hassan, the burden of leadership and uniting the believers fell upon the shoulders of Hussain who accepted his duties wholeheartedly. Hussain was well aware that the religion of Islam had always been based on heroism and sacrifices of kin and blood. Hence when the test of times came, Hussain was ready and willing to lead the people towards the truth and to save Islam even at the cost of his life and that of his family's.

Muawiyah made an oath to Hassan that after his death, Hussain will be the true leader of the Muslim nation. However, when it was time to hand over responsibilities to Hussain, Muawiyah chose his son Yazid as the next leader. This led to one of the biggest battles in the history of this religion. Yazid demanded that Hussain and his people pledge allegiance to him but Hussain knew that Yazid was in the wrong hence he refused. The people abandoned Hussain out of fear but he remained steadfast in his decision to defend his faith at all costs.

The trajectory of events at Karbala are known to us all: man after man was slaughtered and brutally murdered by the army of Yazíd who had rendered Hussain and his followers as traitors and ordered his army to kill them all. Hussain knew of the fate that his followers, his family and even he himself were to face but he knew that he could not surrender to a tyrant. Hussain's sacrifices kept the religion alive and thriving. Hussain was fearless, brave and steadfast.

Hussain took a stand against Yazíd's evil rule. Whilst Yazíd was feared and hated for his ruthlessness, Hussain was loved and respected by society. Yazíd realized this, and understood that if he could convince Hussain to support him, the people would too.

Hussain had a choice. To support the tyrant and live a comfortable life full of luxury, or to refuse and likely be killed for his decision. What should he do? What would you or I do? For Hussain he could not live his life as a supporter of tyranny, and the choice for him was simple. Hussain refused. He said "I only desire to spread good values and prevent evil."

Having refused to support Yazíd, Hussaín knew his life was in danger. Yazíd did not allow anyone to oppose him, and adopted a policy of killing those who disagreed with him. Cautious of this, Hussaín decided to leave his hometown of Medína, and take his family Mecca.

Mecca, the capital city of Islam and home to the Ka'ba, Hussaín hoped Yazíd would respect the holy city and not follow Hussaín and his family. However, Yazíd did not. Forced to leave Mecca, Hussaín set course for Kufa. A city in Iraq where he had received letters of support from. Yazíd predicted this and sent a huge army to block Hussaín from reaching Kufa, and force them to the desert town of Karbala.

Once they reached Karbala, Hussaín with his family 72 companions were surrounded by Yazíd's forces of up to 30,000 men. Despite being hugely outnumbered and with limited access to water, Hussaín refused to give up. Yazíd gave Hussaín a final choice. To either support the government, or be killed.

After receiving the final ultimatum from Yazid, Hussain realized he would be killed in a matter of days. Hussain gathered his companions and urged them to escape. He explained that it was him who Yazid wished to kill, and not them. Again, Hussain's selflessness shone through. Having been deprived of water in the hot desert, he urged his supporters to save themselves.

Despite this, Hussain's men stayed loyal to him and stayed true to their principles. Within a few days Yazid ordered his army to kill Hussain and his companions. When the dust settled, Hussain and his companions were killed. Throughout the forces of Yazid promised him he could leave freely if he chooses to support Yazid, but every time Hussain refused and was eventually killed, holding firmly to his principles.

After his death, Hussain's family were taken captive. His sister, Zainab, took up the role of leadership and gave an inspiring speech in Yazid's palace, condemning his actions and his style of leadership.

Zainab was one of the first to be inspired by Hussain's stand and his principles. Despite the sexism that existed in society at the time, she refused to be silent and held Yazid and his ministers to account for their role in the moral decay of society.

Hussain's example is that one man can stand against an army, and in giving his life inspire those after him to overthrow the abusive Umayyad dynasty. Just as those who lived in the 7th century were inspired by Hussain's stand.

## Hadíth on the vírtues of acquíring knowledge

There are many evidence and vírtues of seeking, acquiring and spreading the knowledge of the deen that can be found in the hadíth of Allah's last messenger Mohammad (ﷺ). Here are some of them:

Abu Huraíra reported Allah's Messenger (ﷺ) as saying:

(When) the time would draw close to the Last Hour, knowledge would be snatched away, turmoil would be rampant, miserliness would be put (in the hearts of the people) and there would be much bloodshed.

– Sahíh Muslím 157 d

2. Abu Mas'ud al-Ansari reported Allah's Messenger (ﷺ) as saying:

The one who is most versed in Allah's Book should act as Imam for the people, but if they are equally versed in reciting it, then the one who has most knowledge regarding Sunnah if they are equal regarding the Sunnah, then the earliest one to emigrate; it they emigrated at the same time, then the earliest one to embrace Islam. No man must lead another in prayer where (the latter) has authority, or sit in his place of honor in his house, without his permission. Ashajj in his narration used the word, "age" in place of "Islam".

– Sahih Muslim 673 a

3. Narrated `Abdullah bin `Umar:

I heard Allah's Messenger (ﷺ) saying, "While I was sleeping, I saw that a cup full of milk was brought to me and I drank of it and gave the remaining of it to `Umar bin Al-Khattab."

They asked. What have you interpreted (about the dream)? O Allah's Messenger (ﷺ)?" The Prophet (ﷺ) said. "(It is Religious) knowledge."

– Sahih al-Bukhari 7032

4. Narrated Ibn `Abbas:

The Prophet (ﷺ) embraced me and said, "O Allah! Teach him (the knowledge of) the Book (Qur'an)."

– Sahih al-Bukhari 7270

5. Narrated Ibn Mas`ud:

"I heard the Prophet (ﷺ) saying, "There is no envy except in two: a person who Allah has given wealth and he spends it in the right way, and a person whom Allah has given wisdom (i.e. religious knowledge) and he gives His decisions accordingly and teaches it to the others." – Sahih al-Bukhari 1409

6. Abu Hurairah reported the Prophet (ﷺ) as saying:

If anyone pursues a path in search of knowledge, Allah will then by make easy for him a path to paradise; and he who is made slow by his actions will not be speeded by his genealogy.

– Sunan Abi Dawud 3643

7. Narrated Habib ibn Maslamah al-Fihri:

Makhul said: I was the slave of a woman of Banu Hudhayl; afterwards she emancipated me. I did not leave Egypt until I had acquired all the knowledge that seemed to me to exist there.

I then came to al-Hijaz and I did not leave it until I had acquired all the knowledge that seemed to be available.

Then I came to al-Iraq, and I did not leave it until I had acquired all the knowledge that seemed to be available.

I then came to Syria, and besieged it. I asked everyone about giving rewards from the booty. I did not find anyone who could tell me anything about it.

I then met an old man called Ziyad ibn Jariyah at-Tamimi. I asked him: Have you heard anything about giving rewards from the booty? He replied: Yes. I heard Maslamah al-Fihri say: I was present with the Prophet (ﷺ).

He gave a quarter of the spoils on the outward journey and a third on the return journey.

– Sunan Abi Dawud 2750

8. Abu Mas'ud narrated that:

Allah's Messenger said: "The one who recites most of the Book of Allah is to lead the people (in prayers.) If they are equal in recitation, then the most knowledgeable in the Sunnah among them. If they are equal regarding the Sunnah, then the earliest of them to emigrate. If they are equal in their emigration then the eldest among them. And a man is not to be led in prayer in the place of his authority, and his spot of esteem in his home is not to be sat on without his permission."

– Jami` at-Tirmidhi 235

9. Abu Hurairah (May Allah be pleased with him) reported:

The Messenger of Allah (ﷺ) said, "The world, with all that it contains, is accursed except for the remembrance of Allah that which pleases Allah; and the religious schools and seekers of knowledge." – At- Tirmidhi, Riyad as-Salihin Book 13, Hadith 9

10. Abu Hurairah narrated that the Messenger of Allah (saw) said:

"Indeed the world is cursed. What is in it is cursed, except for remembrance of Allah, what is conducive to that, the knowledgeable person and the learning person."

– Jami` at-Tirmidhi 2322

11. Hisham bin Hassan narrated from Al-Hasan:

Concerning the saying of Allah: O our Lord, give us good in this world, and good in the Hereafter. He said: "Knowledge and worship in this world, and Paradise in the Hereafter."

– Jami` at-Tirmidhi 3488

## 12. Narrated Yazíd bin 'Umairah:

"When death was upon Mu'adh bin Jabal, it was said to him: 'O Abu' Abdur-Rahman, advise us. ' He said: 'Sit me up.' So he said: 'Indeed, knowledge and faith are at their place, which desires them shall find them.' He said that three times. 'And seek knowledge from four men:' Uwaimír Abu Ad-Darda, with Salman Al-Farísí, with 'Abdullah bin Mas'ud, and with' Abdullah bin Salam who used to be a Jew and then accepted For indeed, I heard the Messenger of Allah (ﷺ) saying, "Indeed he is the tenth of ten in Paradise."

– Jamí` at-Tirmidhí, Vol. 1, Book 46, Hadith 3804

## 13. Narrated Qais Ibn Kathir:

"A man from Al-Madínah came to Abu Ad-Darda when he was in Dimashq. He replied: 'A Hadith reached me which you have narrated from the Messenger of Allah (ﷺ).' He said: 'You did not come for some need?' He said: 'No.'

He said: 'Did you come for trade?' He said: 'No, I did not come except seeking this Hadith.' So he said: 'Indeed, I heard the Messenger of Allah (ﷺ) saying: "Who takes a path upon which he seeks knowledge, then Allah makes a path to Paradise easy for him. And indeed the angels lower their wings in approval to the one seeking knowledge. Indeed forgiveness is ought for the knowledgeable one by whomever is in the heavens and whomever is in the earth, even the fish in the waters. And the superiority of the scholar over the worshiper is like the superiority of the moon over the rest of the celestial bodies. Indeed the scholars are the heirs of the Prophets, and the Prophets do not leave behind Dinar or Dirham. The only legacy of the scholars is knowledge, so whoever takes from it, then he has indeed taken the most able share.

– Jami` at-Tirmidhi 2682

14. Narrated Abu Hurairah:

The Messenger of Allah (ﷺ) said: "Whoever takes a path upon which to obtain knowledge, Allah makes the path to Paradise easy for him."

– Jami` at-Tirmidhi 2646

15. Narrated Anas bin Malik:

The Messenger of Allah (ﷺ) said: "Who goes seeking knowledge, then he is in Allah's cause until he returns."

– Jami` at-Tirmidhi 2647

16. Abu Hurairah, may Allah be pleased with him, narrated that the Messenger of Allah (ﷺ) said:

"When a person dies, his deeds are cut off except for three: Continuing charity, knowledge that others benefited from, and a righteous son who supplicates for him.

– Jami` at-Tirmidhi 1376

17. It was narrated that Ibn 'Abbas said:

"The messenger of Allah said: 'One Faqíh (knowledgeable man) is more formidable against the Shaitan than one thousand devoted worshipers.'"

– Sunan Ibn Majah, Vol. 1, Book 1, Hadíth 222

18. It was narrated from Abu Hurairah that:

The Prophet said: "The best of charity is when a Muslim man gains knowledge, then he teaches it to his Muslim brother."

– Sunan Ibn Majah, Vol. 1, Book 1, Hadíth 243

19. It was narrated that Abu Umamah said:

The Messenger of Allah said: "You must acquire this knowledge before it is taken away." He joined his middle finger and the one that next to the thumb like this, and said: "The scholar and the seeker of knowledge will share the reward, and there is no good in the rest of the people."

– Sunan Ibn Majah, Vol. 1, Book 1, Hadith 228

20. Sahl bin Mu'adh bin Anas narrated from his father that:

The Prophet said: "Whoever teaches some knowledge will have the reward of the one who acts upon it, without that detracting from his reward in the slightest."

– Sunan Ibn Majah, Vol. 1, Book 1, Hadith 240

21. It was narrated from Umm Salamah that when the Prophet (ﷺ) performed the Subh (Morning Prayer), while he said the Salam, he would say:

"Allahumma inni as'aluka' ilman nafi'an, wa rizqan tayyiban, wa 'amalan mutaqabbalan (O Allah, I ask You for beneficial knowledge, good provision and acceptable deeds)."

– Sunan of Ibn Majah, Vol. 1, Book 5, Hadith 925

22. It was narrated from Anas bin Malik that the Messenger of Allah (ﷺ) said:

"Seeking knowledge is a duty upon every Muslim, and he who passes knowledge to those who do not deserve it, is like one who puts a necklace of jewels, pearls and gold around the neck of swines."

– Sunan of Ibn Majah, Vol. 1, Book 1, Hadith 224

Share and get your reward in the akhírah!

## Good Reads

* Don't Be Sad! Be Happy!          ISBN: 9781643544878
* Stories of the Prophets          ISBN: 9798774942602
* The Ideal Muslimah               ISBN: 9798834334422
* Hadiths on Good Moral            ISBN: 9781643544823
* Matters of the Heart             ISBN: 9781643544731
* The Battles of Prophet           ISBN: 9781643544724
* Stories of the Qur'an            ISBN: 9781643544700
* Timeless Seeds of Advice         ISBN: 9781643544694
* Tafsir Ibn Kathir                ISBN: 9781643544625
* The Lofty Virtues of             ISBN:  9781643544601
* Inner Dimensions of Salah        ISBN: 9781643544571
* The Journey of the Spirit        ISBN: 9781643544496
* Al-Husain Ibn Ali                ISBN: 9781643544328
* The Friends of Allah             ISBN: 9781643544236
* Gardens of Purification          ISBN: 9781643544229
* The Spiritual Cure               ISBN: 9781643544212
* Fleeing From the Fire            ISBN: 9781643544205
* The Journey of the Strangers     ISBN: 9781643544175
* The Heavenly Dispute             ISBN: 9781643544168

* Disciplining the Soul　　　　　ISBN: 9781643544151
* Life in al-Barzakh　　　　　　ISBN: 9781643544144
* Diseases of the Hearts　　　　ISBN: 9781643544106
* The Path To Guidance　　　　ISBN: 9781643544052
* Miracles of the Prophet　　　ISBN: 9781643544038
* Al-Fawaid: A Collection of　　ISBN: 9781643543789
* Great Women　　　　　　　　ISBN: 9781643543772
* The Story of Muhammad　　　ISBN: 9781643543635
* Thirty Lessons for those Fast　ISBN: 9781643543628
* Seerat of Prophet　　　　　　ISBN: 9781643543611
* WhasWasa: The Whispering　　ISBN: 9781643543499
* Khalid Bin Al-Waleed　　　　　ISBN: 9781643543444
* The Islamic Jesus　　　　　　ISBN:  9781643543376
* The Spiritual Path to Allah　　ISBN: 9781643544885
* Things We Don't Talk About in Islam ISBN: 9781643544960

www.ingramcontent.com/pod-product-compliance
Lightning Source LLC
Chambersburg PA
CBHW071905070526
44583CB00016B/1846